We Didn't Come Here to Stay

Race, Religion & Reflections

POETRY by **Elmer Beard**
The Octo Griot

We Didn't Come Here to Stay.

Copyright © 2024 . First Edition.

All rights reserved. No part of this publication may be reproduced, distributed or transmitted in any form or by any means, including photocopying, recording, or other electronic or mechanical methods, including photocopying, recording, or any information storage and retrieval system now known or to be invented, without the prior written permission of the publisher, except in the case of brief quotations embodied in critical reviews and certain other noncommercial uses permitted by copyright law. For permission requests, write to the publisher, addressed "Attention: Permissions Coordinator," at the address below.

Library of Congress Cataloging-in-Publication Data
Beard, Elmer
We Didn't Come Here to Stay / by Elmer Beard
Front and Back Cover photographer: Sonya Beard

Library of Congress Control Number: 2020911713
978-1-7352975-8-3 - paperback
978-1-7352975-9-0 - hardcover

Registration has been applied for at the United States Copyright Office.
Published in the United States of America
Freedom's Price Publishing
P.O. Box 1105
Hot Springs, Arkansas 71902
freedomsprice1863@gmail.com

To my late siblings Torbett, Pauline, Selmarie, Marbalene and Luther Bennie Jr.

CONTENTS

ACKNOWLEDGMENTS ix
PRAYER-LOGUE xiii

Three Hots and a Cot 1
Heat Wave 2
The Streams 3
Campaign Rally 4
Bill and Jimmy 5
The Greater Good 6
A Prayer for All People 7
When You Retire 8

AUSTRALIA 10
Mother Dear 12
Delayed Birth Certificate 13
Night Weeping 14
You Oughta Pray 15
Notes from the Delta 16
Blackville 17
My First Dog 18
Rusty 19

SOUTH AMERICA 20
How America Got Great 22
After the Tears 23
Determination 24

Pointless Point 25
Home Salon 26
Corner Store 27
Culture Consumption 28
Love Offering 29

ASIA 30
Malcolm Laughed 32
Martin Spoke 33
Alma Matters 34
In the Real World. 35
Crazy Uncle. 36
Forgiving Prayer. 37
High On Hope 38
Side Effects 39

EUROPE 40
Summer's Peak. 42
April and October 43
Seemed Like Yesterday 44
Only the Date Has Changed 45
Come On, Choir 46
A Disturbing Noise 47
Necessities of Life 48
Platinum Years. 49

AFRICA. 50
Golden School Days. 52
Board of Education 53

Sacred Platform 54
Pastoral Standards. 55
The Wink. 56
Peep Holes 57
Peace in Knowing. 58
Paths Unknown 59

ASIA 60
Creatures. 62
Clutter Bug 63
Precious Name 64
Your Kingdom 65
In the Kitchen. 66
The Colored Broom 67
Read Something. 68
The Definition 69

SOUTH AMERICA. 70
Even Days 72
Let Your Light 73
Them Hogs 74
Holiday Meat 75
Communication Rules. 76
Declaration 77
Relocation. 78
Hope for the Hood. 79

EUROPE 80
Morning Chores 82

Nightmares 83
A New Dog 84
That Old Cat 85
Out of the Box. 86
In Lieu Of 87
Mother Big Oak 88
Chopping Block 89

AFRICA 90
Magnetism 92
Brief Separation 93
Our People 94
You People 95
Pay Your Debts. 96
Underground Banking. 97
Penal Systems. 98
Without Cameras 99

NORTH AMERICA 100
Well Water 102
My Mules and Me 103
Call My Name. 104
Don't Call Me Bud 105
Ode to a Landmark 106
Future Plans 108
Around the Casket 109

BIO 111

ACKNOWLEDGMENTS

Years ago, I was talking to an old acquaintance about a list of people whose journeys in this life had come to an end. As I lamented about the losses, he uttered a simple, southern yet profound statement: "We Didn't Come Here to Stay."

The thought caused me to confront my own mortality. I was reminded of how short our journeys were on this Earth. We're travelers, merely passing through, along life's way. We're headed to the great unknown—or in my case—my eternal home.

The thought also caused me to confront my own vitality. I'm reminded of all the journeys I've taken around the world. As a traveler, I've been blessed to visit sites on six continents. Often, I think about how to make the most of my remaining time.

No matter our age, we should live each day as if it were our last.

I spend most of my days writing about and reflecting on my 87 years of life that have been abundant in blessings and wealthy in opportunities. I have outlived two wives, all of my siblings and too many friends to name. I continue to be what has been described by my three adult children as "the best Dad." I have owned more than 20 hogs, about 10 dogs, a few mules and horses, and chickens.

Some of these folks and creatures have been featured in my works, which over the decades have included more than a thousand documents scribbled on yellow legal pads. Some of those stories are immortalized here in my second volume of poetry titled, *We Didn't Come Here to Stay*.

Since my debut poetry collection, *Let Reason Roll: Race, Religion & Reflections*, there has been no cure for the highly contagious disease of racism. The social, spiritual and mental illness continues to be a major theme in my life and this work. I fear things will not change until Christ returns.

I will always love Dorothy Beard, my wife of 40 years, for making me a better man, bearing my children and telling my daughters to care for me upon her departure. Her loss left me feeling empty inside, so I rekindled my love affair with writing as a way of healing to fulfill the void.

I would like to thank my older daughter for being my primary caretaker, turning off the stove behind me, waking me up from horrific nightmares and resuming my civic work in the community.

My younger daughter, a professional editor, has assisted with selecting, excerpting, transcribing, formatting and removing the names to protect the innocent in this latest poetry collection.

Many people are surprised that I have a son, so I wanted to acknowledge him here. He is my first born and I am proud of him.

I also want to thank my second wife, Wilhelmina Franklin Beard. I appreciate her children and family for continuing to support me after her passing.

To the pastor, deacons and congregants of the Roanoke Baptist Church, I appreciate your encouragement and continued support in all my endeavors.

To the nation's oldest civil rights organization, the NAACP, I salute you. Unit #6013 has always been a torchbearer for justice and equality for our community.

I am forever grateful for my longtime typist and spelling wiz Ms. Ann Works, who typed more than 400 drafts for me before retiring. I also appreciate Adrienne Conley and Esther Dixon for typing drafts of my later work.

I'd like to thank the Hot Springs Poet Laureate Kai Coggins, who hosts Wednesday Night Poetry, the nation's longest-running weekly open-mic poetry series.

Publisher John Archibald at Muscadine Press was instrumental in the early stages of my journey, and I thank him to this day.

Dave Richards has strengthened the quality of my work and understood my rage in certain selections of poetry. He has always been a huge supporter of my craft.

Willie "Scorehack" Perkins has encouraged me and urged me not to delay the publication during these troubled times. He has reminded me of the old days.

This work has been enriched by my experience in presenting speeches at my local Toastmasters club each week.

Again, I want to thank my Lord for the passion, time, patience and mind to write. It has been good therapy, which has helped to manage my anger and calm my restlessness while I navigate a world that does not always love me back the way You do, Lord.

PRAYER-LOGUE

Dear Lord,

Thank You, Father, for sparing me to live and thrive on this Earth for four score and seven years. You have blessed me to reach my platinum age and enjoy the surplus of my life.

Lord, I thank You for my traveling mercies that have guided and protected me throughout life's journey and world adventures. Thank You for my strong limbs that allow me to walk for miles a day and flexible fingers that allow me to write as I win the painful battle against arthritis.

Thanks for letting me live to see the publication of my second volume of poetry. I plan to write until my dying day, but I have too much to say for one lifetime. I will focus on completing the next page, chapter or volume.

I thank You in advance and praise You on credit for all the blessings that have been my wonderful life.

Father, I pray in the name of Your Son Jesus, a Brotha from Bethlehem.

Amen.

Three Hots and a Cot

Keep count of every crime committed
Three strikes could be your last shot
When you get locked up in the system
You're looking at three hots and a cot

When you are convicted of a felony
Forever changed your life will be
If it were one hundred years earlier
You might be hanging from a tree

Now you commit a misdemeanor
Because you need a place to squat
In the joint some things are certain
You'll have three hots and a cot

Heat Wave

Slowly you came in on your own time
Steadily you held your burning wave
Mercilessly the sun came beating down
Brightly you shone for countless days

Little rain has fallen in several weeks
Starting this pattern shortly after May
The wave set in for short periods of time
Historic records you tied day after day

Extreme temps took a toil on humankind
A brutal climate caused many to retreat
It baked the Earth so it couldn't breathe
Causing many to die in the scorching heat

The Streams

On the 40 acres of land that we owned
Live streams were tucked under the hills
Hidden in trees, weeds, bushes and vines

One of our streams was used for a spring
Where we fetched pails of water as needed

Drinkers could barely taste its natural deposits
That would stain a glass jar over some time

After three or four trips to the stream
We could fill a 10-gallon steel washpot
Set a fire underneath to boil the water
And add bits of soap and lye to do laundry

Laundry water was perfect for evening baths
Fresh water that was used to rinse the laundry
Rinsed the soap and lye from our bodies

We were as purified as the clothes we wore

Campaign Rally

You can sit down and do nothing
Or point fingers and complain

Come up with the same old excuses
Wait for someone else to lead

Or seek public office
And change the world

All runners are winners
Even if they lose the race

All winners are runners
Victory comes in competing

Struggling in freedom's fight
Is always worth the costly price

You have a responsibility
To be the revolution

Bill and Jimmy

As a city councilman, I had a special assignment in 1971.
I waited at the Municipal Airport for Peanut One to land.

The Arkansas Attorney General introduced me to the
Governor of Georgia.

I was assigned to be a chauffeur in the motorcade.
I drove the decoy, a black government car, to the
Convention Center.

The governor was traveling in front of me in a beige car.

There were no incidents that day.

However, more than 50 years later, I realized something.
A historical moment had taken place.

I had been introduced to the
Future 39th President of the United States by the
Future 42nd President of the United States.

Though none of us knew it then.

The Greater Good

Why do we do the things we do
And say the things that we say?
It may be out of character for us
When we act in a certain way?

Why are we careful with our words
Mindful of how much we reveal?
Why is it best that some don't know
The true manner of how we feel?

If issues turn out to be bigger than us
Can we look at the bigger picture too?
Why doesn't everyone realize that
Advancing the group includes you?

Why are our responses hypocritical
Instead of saying the things we should?
Sometimes diplomacy is better served
When we consider the greater good.

A Prayer for All People

Prepare Your people for whatever
You have in store for us

Enlighten us with understanding
So we will not question Your will

Continue to shower us with blessings
That You have bestowed on us

Build a fence around us for protection
When we are vulnerable

Comfort us through our suffering
To remind us You make no mistakes

Lead us in the path of righteousness
As You would have us to go

Encourage us as we continue to travel
To our eternal home with Thee

When You Retire ...

1. Thank the Lord for reaching your retirement
2. Sign up for an aqua aerobics class
3. Make a new friend without a self-serving motive
4. Learn to say "Hello" in five different languages
5. Ask for discounts from major retailers, hotels and restaurants
6. Vote early in every election and drive voters to the polls
7. Update your wardrobe
8. Visit someone you know (or don't know) in a nursing home
9. Paint the house, patio or fence
10. Consider ways you can help eliminate racism
11. Read one Bible chapter per week
12. Volunteer with children at an underfunded school
13. Take up a yoga class
14. Wear your natural hair color and let your gray shine
15. Travel to a different country
16. Forgive five people who have wronged you (including yourself)
17. Become tech-savvy
18. Join the NAACP and attend their monthly meetings
19. Visit someone in prison or jail
20. Renew your vows
21. Follow a recipe to make a healthy new dish
22. Attend an African-American church
23. Create a family scholarship fund
24. Tell your children you love them (even if it's awkward)
25. Pray every morning, noonday and evening

26. Record or write the story of your life
27. Take daily or biweekly walks
28. Ask five women how you could help eliminate misogyny
29. Do something to beautify your neighborhood
30. Get regular deep-tissue massages
31. Make a list of foods for senior citizens to avoid
32. Reconnect with old schoolmates
33. Buy products in bulk and share with the less fortunate
34. Babysit for an exhausted parent
35. Visit national parks across the country
36. Donate to a Historically Black College or University
37. Participate in cemetery cleanups
38. Jot down five positive things about the worst person you know
39. Grow or shave your beard
40. Hug your adult children (even if it's awkward)
41. Document interesting events on social media
42. Trace your family history back as far as you can
43. Run errands for the elderly or people with disabilities
44. Work on a local political campaign
45. Read five books written by African-American authors
46. Sign up for a self-defense class
47. Clean out your attic, garage or storage room
48. Submit a letter to the editor at your local newspaper
49. Cross off items on your Bucket List
50. Get some rest and drink lots of water

AUSTRALIA
Sydney Opera House
Sydney, Australia

Elmer Beard
Enjoying an afternoon in Circular Quay

Mother Dear

She spent years of her adult life
Extending our family branch
Most attempts were successful
Filling our home with children

With a total of eight expectations
Bearing four girls and four boys
With a stillborn son and daughter
Exiting this life before they entered

Her last labor caused the greatest pain
Waiting on a doctor to become sober
She endured with no medical assistance
Failing to survive the complicated delivery

Childbirth should bring the joys of life
Bringing women, instead, close to death
That was the final task of my dear mother
Extending the branch of our family tree

Delayed Birth Certificate

I was born Negro in 1937

It was early in the evening

The location was listed as Route 2

There was no mention of any hospital

Most Negroes weren't born in hospitals then

There weren't any Negro hospitals in our community

Negroes were born at home on rural routes with midwives

I had no formal record of my birth until I was an adult

Then I needed to apply for my Social Security card

I had to get official documentation at age 19

To get my first job to save up for college

I got a Delayed Birth Certificate

Which came many years

After my birth

Night Weeping

Weeping will come
More in the night
Than in the day

Weeping in silence
Leads to sin of worry
When it's dark and quiet

We've taken on our own
Life's load of problems
Bearing the burden

Understanding not
The mind can't stop racing
The heart and soul ache

Eyes soak absorbent pillows
After the weeping ceases
And both eyes are dry

It is then a new day begins

You Oughta Pray

Your prayer

Oughta be fitting

Oughta be heartfelt

Oughta be considerate

Oughta be well-structured

Oughta be grammatically correct

Oughta be an appropriate amount of time

If your prayer falls short of any of these suggestions

You oughta pray anyway

Notes from the Delta

Across the plantation

In a few hours

The fields flooded

Yesterday, I saw land

Today, I see only water

It's now a shallow lake

Tractors are parked and idled

White bosses watch the clock

Black field hands take a break

Engrossed in various games

Until the water recedes

Blackville

There was a man

Born enslaved

Became free

Worked hard

Secured wealth

Incorporated a town

Called it Blackville

Started churches

Opened schools

Purchased real estate

Farmed the land

Hired Blacks and whites

Earned a pilot's license

Owned an airplane

Parked it at his airport

All in the late 1800s

That man was Pickens Black

My First Dog

Trailer was my very first dog.
He would trail my siblings and me
Every time we left the house.
We would tell him to go home.

He would wait until we got out of view.
And then he would catch up with us.

One day, someone apparently shot him.
The gunshot left a bullet wound in his shoulder.
It didn't kill him though.

Years went by.

Trailer died at an old age with a limp.

Rusty

Our dog Rusty, whose color was reflected in his name, was stolen.

Or he ran away.

Or he was hit by a car.

I'm not sure exactly what happened to him.

It was the fourth Sunday in September.

I remember the day but not the year.

I just know we never saw old Rusty again.

SOUTH AMERICA
Avenida Cristobal Colón
Santiago, Chile

Elmer Beard
Posing with Rapa Nui statues

How America Got Great

How did America get so great?
It was in the shipping business

Importing stolen goods across the Atlantic
Smuggling human cargo

It was a system of commodities
Bred like cattle, sold like crops

On the human stock exchange
It was the best return on investment

High profits, no payroll, no overhead
Free and forced labor

It was a whitewashed history of denial
Filled with ignorance and omissions

Burying truth in America's untold stories
From 1619 to 1865
To today ... the lies continue.

After the Tears

Our tears reflect our love
They reveal our inward desire for perfection
A need for human improvement
Uncomfortable we become
But after our tears ...
Problems remain forever
Noticeably unchanged
Our tears dry and fade and vanish
As we smile and grin and joke
A few sincere questions
With answers and solutions
We want change without action
Though we see a need for others to act
Maybe we can begin
To change our world
Slowly but steadily
After the tears

Determination

We must make a difference
But it may not count now
Though our lives be brief
We'll be determined somehow

The voiceless who do not speak
Will be heard loud and clear
The gutless who do not march
Will boldly strut with no fear

We'll be determined somehow
May make no difference at all
Still standing up for what is just
Still rising every time we fall

Pointless Point

Opinion becomes truth
Repeatedly we contend
Voices elevate to the extreme
No additional information
Just the same old verbiage
Too many personal experiences
Once pointed conversation
Now rambling discourse
Losing points with each breath
Previously opened ears
Eventually begin to close
When the intended point
Starts to diminish and fade
Begin a conclusion
Summarize your point
Before it becomes pointless

Home Salon

Women enter the house and head toward the rear
High-pitched murmurs of gossip catch their ear

They walk on back through a blinding thick haze
Smoke clouds, oil sheen and setting sprays

Familiar scents of fruity shampoos fill the air
But nothing smells stronger than deep-fried hair

Pressing combs and curling irons on high heat
Determined to take down kinky naps in defeat

Scalps doused with harsh chemicals and hot grease
Extreme measures taken to control hair with ease

Tender care and steady hands calmed any fears
Creating standards of beauty throughout the years

From conventional 'dos and individual styles
Satisfied clients always leave wearing smiles

Corner Store

At the Corner Store for Colored
They were the days of yesterday
The prices were excessively high
They knew when we got our pay

At the Corner Store for Colored
They had our general needs in stock
They were located down dusty roads
Or sometimes the middle of the block

At the Corner Store for Colored
Once a month we settled the bill
Then shopped year-round on credit
Waiting 'til Christmas to get a deal

At the Corner Store for Colored
Quality and expectations were low
We were reluctant loyal customers
'Cause we had no other place to go

Culture Consumption

Uplifted spirit

Avoided a life of dullness

Denounced boredom

Climbing always upward

With more smiles than tears

From native instincts

Under no patterned practice

Above normal expectations

No mold in existence

To the surprise of the masses

For the world to consume

Love Offering

Savings account closed

Running low

Cup half-empty

Wiped out, tapped out

Just paid the tithes

Scraping the bottom of the barrel

Drained, spent, busted

Extended all extensions

Month-to-month

Financial distress again

Share the burden

Give what your heart desires

Collect a love offering

ASIA
Baptismal Site of Jesus Christ
Al-Maghtas, Jordan

Elmer Beard
Going to be baptized in the River Jordan

Malcolm Laughed

I believe the year was 1963
At the University of Wisconsin
There had been a presentation
Speaking on matters new to us

Our guest traveled with an entourage
Of Black men in bowties and nice suits

He made his way to the lobby
Of our graduate living quarters
The hallways began to overflow
I was pushed farther up the stairs
Just beyond the arguing distance

I still saw him

Young, sharp and smooth

And I heard him

One by one, students began
Introducing themselves
"... Jones, Williams, Jenkins ..."
Malcolm X laughed at them, saying
"I see none of you know your real names."

Martin Spoke

As a young college English professor, I had the chance
to hear one of the greatest speakers to ever walk this Earth.

He spoke about sharing a pulpit with his father at a
Baptist church in Atlanta.

He discussed where he was, how he got there and
where he was going. He addressed pressing problems
and presented resolutions to those problems.

He spoke so eloquently.

He was a wizard of literary devices. During the 20-minute address,
he used more than 70 figures of speech. Personification, similes and
metaphors … He sounded like a writer but he spoke with no notes.

Listening to him I couldn't help but wonder what would become of
his future.

He had already been jailed several times.
His house had been bombed, too.

Many of us were whispering, "They're going to get him."

And they did.

Alma Matters

From friends and a few alumni
Who graduate, return and share
Well-planned monthly meetings
Much time and money they spare

Private and public funds are raised
Folks donate as much as they can
Always cheerful in their contributions
Our Alma Mater is in great demand

We solicit those with deep pockets
Even small gifts can be a blessing
It's better to give than receive
Is our greatest college lesson

In the Real World

Where perfection counts
Where lethargy is eliminated
Where ignorance is abandoned
In the real world

Excuses are now tolerated
Memories are now selective
Laziness is beyond weakness
In the real world

Laws should be checked
Society must be balanced
Life has not ever been fair
In the real world

Crazy Uncle

He had a good woman

He had a baby girl

He had a hatchet

He chopped her into pieces

He was declared insane

He went to prison for years

He was finally released

He got his life together

He bought a trailer and truck

He ate BBQ goat and pork

He drank cheap whiskey

He died in a nursing home

He was buried in a box

By a forgiving daughter

With no mother

Forgiving Prayer

Dear Jesus,

I call on Your holy name at this hour. Please forgive me for the commandments I have broken and continue to break. I have failed in more ways than I can remember. Only You know each one of my sins, and only You can forgive me.

When I'm deceived by others who use me for their selfish needs, Lord, help me to keep my eyes on You. Now, Father, those who choose to lie on me as I have lied on others, please forgive them. I also forgive those who have wronged me.
They, like me, are Yours, too.

Heavenly Father, remind us, Your sinful children, that we have all come short of Your glory. We have our strengths and weaknesses even when we do the best we can. For that forgiving spirit that only You can impart to me, I'll forever be grateful to You, My Lord.

Take me back to the story of the cross where You hanged, bled, died and rose again so that we may be forgiven. Save my sinful soul in order that I may have eternal life someday.

I'll Stay in Touch,

Your Favorite Child

High On Hope

At the School of Hard Knocks
We majored in hope

We knew we were poor
But we were rich in spirit

Tough times would set in
But life would get better

During our darkest days
We always kept the faith

At our lowest moments
We were high on hope

Side Effects

Instilled by lecturing and disciplining
Some teachings corrupt the student
In mentally destructive classrooms

Out-of-context messages are taken
Some actions were never intended
Straying far from the topic at hand
Failing to announce digressions

Illuminating, wavering, damaging
Warpness occurs in the process
Detrimental side effects linger

EUROPE
The Eiffel Tower
Paris, France

Elmer Beard
Touring iconic sites along the River Seine

Summer's Peak

Now it's August in the South
As expected, it's hot and sunny
Just fewer than a hundred degrees
With few puffs of clouds above

Noticeable breezes ripple and flow
A month of complaint-free days
Once again, summer is at its peak
And autumn is a season away

April and October

April and October, the mildest months of all
When temperatures are at their calmest
They begin the Spring and the Fall

April is the annual celebration of my birth
It's a time to plow and a time to plant
Moment to measure one's worth

October is the annual celebration of my wife
It's a time to harvest the fruits of labor
As she labored to birth new life

Seemed Like Yesterday

Caroline was uncertain of her age. She knew she was anywhere from 10 to 15 years old when Lincoln signed the freedom papers.

One of her vivid memories was serving dinner at the main house.
She was walking to the table with a bowl of squash.
She never made it to the table. The squash fell to the floor.

The master whipped her so severely that she remembered the lashing well into her old age when she shared the experience with her great-great-grandchildren.

She would retell the story as if it had happened yesterday.

Only the Date Has Changed

Although the 1960s are long and gone
Systemic oppression is still on the rise
Hidden tactics amid structural barriers
Historically, hatred has been in disguise

Gone are the days of the segregated signs
Colored and white facilities now the same
Discrimination embedded in southern life
It appears that only the date has changed

Old offenses are now microaggressions
Racism is nice, and sometimes it's polite
Results are no less calculated and cruel
Killing the spirit with every little slight

Incarceration rates are at an all-time high
Modern-day slavery taking on a new name
With more spent on prisons than on schools
It's clear that only the date has changed

Increases in poverty exploit communities
Income gaps widened by corporate greed
Wealth disinherited with each generation
Economic inequalities continue to breed

Laws have passed and policies abolished
Decades go by but those attitudes remain
In places where hostile tradition prevails
In the South, only the date has changed

Come On, Choir

Come on! Come on!

Let's go! Can't be late.

We've got rehearsals

We had a good practice

Hurry! Hurry! Hurry!

Line up, line up!

No talking, mouths closed

Take your places

Now call the roll ...

Sopranos, Altos

Tenors, Basses

Raise your heads

Lift your voices

A Disturbing Noise

Settling in for a quiet evening, unwinding

Reflecting and gathering my thoughts

Suddenly, I heard a disturbing noise from outside the house

It was a loud medley of voices, animals and vehicles

The commotion disturbed my peace

People were yelling, a child was crying, car horns were blowing

Every dog in the neighborhood howled and barked in unison

My curiosity got the best of me

I quickly left the comfort of my sofa to investigate the uproar

A man had set his home on fire

His home was an abandoned car on a nearby lot

After the excitement died down, he had to find

New shelter to drink and smoke

And I returned to my evening of peace and quiet

Necessities of Life

Privilege is living in a place where
The little things are taken for granted

The Good Book reminds us of
Your grace and generosity

You have provided food for us
That we did not plant nor raise

You have supplied us with water
From wells that we did not dig

You have draped us in clothes
That we did not manufacture

You have given us shelter
In houses we did not build

Lord, we are thankful every day
For the basic necessities of life

You have showered us
With bountiful blessings

Whether we deserved them or not

Platinum Years

When you become a member
of the Senior Citizen Society
You're given credit for having paid your dues
You take the scenic route of life
You sleep without an alarm
You learn to let things go

When you become a veteran
of the Senior Citizen Society
You're surcharged for exceeding life expectancy
You begin to outlive your friends
You feel your time dwindling
You become less patient

With more years behind you
Than you have in front of you
You may chuckle about
Your declining health
Your jiggling limbs and
Your fading memory

And ask the age-old question:

Do you remember when?

AFRICA
The Pyramids at Giza
Cairo, Egypt

Elmer Beard
Riding a camel in the Sahara

Golden School Days

I attended a two-room schoolhouse with a wood-burning heater and no electricity.

The only facility was a restroom with no running water outback in a shed.

The playground equipment was a rope tied to a Sycamore tree for swinging.

Our drinking fountain was water drawn from a deep well in the center of a dirt field.

Those were our golden school days.

Board of Education

In the summer of 1941, my older sister and I took a trip to the spring for a cool drink of water.

My mother ordered us to go and return without delay.
Our interest in butterflies and wildflowers distracted us too long.
Upon returning, my mother disciplined us. She referred to this punishment as the Board of Education; in fact, it was just a switch from a nearby bush.

The punishment went exactly like this:
"I told you about playing when I sent you to the spring!"

Then she choreographed our spanking with this dare:
"Now. Go. Do. It. Again."
Each of the five words was punctuated with a lick of the switch.

We didn't understand then, like we do now, why mothers told you to do something you weren't supposed to do.

Sacred Platform

Preachers watch your tone
Pulpits are not playgrounds

Comic relief is distracting
End all of the foolishness

Congregants lose focus
Paying spiritual attention

Silly jokes won't improve
Poorly prepared messages

Our souls need to be fed
Our funny bones not tickled

In the sanctuary of praise
God's word is precious

Deliver a good sermon
Instead of a good laugh

Pulpits are sacred platforms
Keep them holy

Pastoral Standards

Should churches establish a code of ethics for ministers of the gospel?

Should pastors be held to a higher moral standard?

Should ministers practice what they preach?

Are there any traits that are disqualifying?

Is it acceptable for a pastor to be single?

Do pastors need traditional families?

Must ministers obtain college degrees?

What credentials are necessary to preach?

Do churches make space for women in leadership?

Do congregations welcome female pastors in the pulpit?

Should churches have a mandatory retirement age for pastors?

What are the tough questions that we're avoiding in the church today?

The Wink

Why do they wink rather than speak?
Is it too much to ask for a simple hello?
It's their way of saying, "I see you,
But you don't merit my speaking to you."
We are acceptable enough to be around them
And we should be glad to be in their presence
They try to be respectful, and
In doing so they disrespect you
They don't address you formally
They just wink
Then they grin and laugh
When nothing is funny
They want to keep us laughing
So we won't make them
Uncomfortable by reminding
Them of the pain that has been inflicted on us
Instead, they should be glad to be in our presence
They have so much to learn from us
Like forgiveness

Peep Holes

She agreed to meet with him
At a certain day and certain hour.
When he stopped by her home
She looked out of the peep hole,
And she noticed the gentleman
Was sporting a shiny bald head.
She just stared and said nothing.

The next day, her gentleman caller
Offered her some friendly advice:
"Lady, the next time someone comes to
Your door to see you, don't look through
The peep hole and pretend not to be home.
While you were looking at me through
The peep hole, I was looking through
The peep hole back at you."

As for myself, I don't do peep holes.

Peace in Knowing

Never wandering or wavering
Always focusing on the infinite
That is the peace in knowing

Knowing what to do at times
When one knows not what to do
Help is only a prayer away

That everlasting peace in knowing
When one has given and granted
When drained and strained

Hope in good times and in bad
At my days' end, peace awaits me
He knows how much we can handle

Heavier is our load day by day
Blessed assurance we have
That peace in knowing God

Paths Unknown

Here you are in your cap and gown
Preparing your life for a new start
Adorned in your scholastic regalia
With honors given from the heart

Learning life lessons is more valuable
Than the official degree you obtained
Perseverance and persistence allowed
Your hopes and dreams to be attained

Overcoming hurdles that blocked your way
It's immeasurable how much you've grown
Trust in God and let Him light your path
Especially when traveling paths unknown

ASIA
Depensar
Bali, Indonesia

Elmer Beard
Exiting a traditional theater

Creatures

Perfect creatures in the wilderness

All through the air they fly free
All that roam through the woods
All that navigate through the sea

Creatures exist outside humankind
Beautiful beasts running in the wild
With no wars, no sins and no crimes

They thirst, they hunger and thrive
Employing their animal instincts
Fighting till their death to survive

Clutter Bug

Pack everything in a desk drawer
Store some things under there
Cover the top with more items
Hang news clippings everywhere

Chairs become makeshift shelves
Corners are crowded with stuff
Only a narrow path for walking
Room for storage is never enough

Cluttering takes up valuable space
Consuming too much valuable time
It overwhelms a room, office or home
And it also clutters your mind

Precious Name

You are the Light of the World
And the Defeater of Darkness

You are the Good Shepherd
And the Holy Lamb

You are the Bread of Life
And the Living Water

You are the King of Kings
And the Prince of Peace

You are our Heavenly Father
And the Son of Man

You are Alpha and Omega
The Beginning and the End

Our Lord and our God
So precious is Your name

Amen.

Your Kingdom

Our Father in Heaven, as You watch over us from Your kingdom,
We do thank You for the countless blessings we now enjoy.

We pray for forgiveness for our sins. May we be reminded
that You are merciful God, and we are imperfect creatures
striving toward perfection.

Please lead us away from the temptation that lurks around us.
And deliver us from evil and the very appearance of evil
that obstructs our pathway.

May Your word be seen in us through the lives we live.
May Your kingdom be our kingdom when our earthly life has ended.

We will forever remain focused on You.
Your power and Your glory is our need and desire.

We pray in the name of Your Son, Jesus, a Negro from Nazareth.

Amen.

In the Kitchen

There's no fellowshipping in the kitchen
Unless you're blessing food with grace
There's room for one designated cook
For two or more, there's not enough space

Consider it a classroom for the culinary arts
Or science lab to experiment with flavors
A workshop to taste the limits of imagination
Whipping up dishes for loved ones to savor

Chatty kitchens cause chaos and confusion
Utensils are scattered everywhere you look
Time needed to get arranged and organized
And concentration is needed for the cook

Review family recipes and prep the food
Fry it up in a pan and then stir up the pot
Direct your guests toward the dining room
Where the getting is good while it's hot

Once the feast is over and your bellies are filled
You've had your last bite and sipped your last sip
Move festivities to the kitchen to thank the chef
Lend a hand with the dishes while you fellowship

The Colored Broom

Shopping while Colored has always been costly.

Back when many Colored folk weren't able to read, they were given written receipts and often charged for a "broom" by white store clerks.

The customers were never sold the "broom;" it was merely added to their bill. Most times, they would walk out of the store without checking the receipt. On rare occasions, a customer would question the charge. In those cases, the white store clerk would appear shocked, remove it from the bill and dismiss it as an honest mistake.

The Colored "broom" took the form of a pot, a fan or some other household item. Whatever it was, the "broom" made more money than any other product, and it never even left the store.

The Colored broom helped to engine the Jim Crow economy.

Read Something

Read anything, anywhere, anytime
Read about ideas, concepts, opinions
Read about people, places, things

Reading
Increases vocabulary
Improves spelling
Decreases boredom

Read a good book
Read a bad book
Read anything

As long as you read something

The Definition

You are Lord
There is no
Comparison

You are the
Son of God
You have no equal

You are the Creator
Of everything
In existence

Before time
Was measured
You were God

No limits
Can be placed
On You in any way

You are
Omnipotent
Omniscient and
Omnipresent

That is the
Definition of God

SOUTH AMERICA
Cristo Redentor
Rio de Janeiro, Brazil

Elmer Beard
Spending a moment at Christ the Redeemer

Even Days

There are no long days or short days
Hours in a day are always the same
The Lord made every day even
Managing that time is to blame

God said, "Let there be light!"
To shine through the atmosphere
Now, lightness and darkness
Differ throughout the year

Our Father who created time
Created the night and the day
Gave us the sun and the moon
With 24 hours to do what we may

Let Your Light

Let Your light
So shine in my life
That I will have no thought
For anything but good

Teach me, O Lord,
To become
A doer of Your
Holy word

Endow me, O Lord,
With the kindness
To influence others
While I'm doing Your will

Guide me, O Lord,
So I may find the solution
To any problem that
I may encounter

Bless me, O Lord,
To be able to overcome
Evil with good

Them Hogs

Slick was one of those hogs that would take off running.
Once Slick broke through the fence and met a formidable foe.
Slick ran into a wild dog and came up short in the match.
Slick had some missing parts—an eye, ear and butt cheek.
Papa healed him and fed him corn to clean out his system.
Then Papa shot him between the eyes and scalded him in boiling water.
Slick still had some missing parts.

Papa suspected that a shoulder had been stolen.
Papa couldn't identify the culprit though.
I said, "Papa, hold on a minute. We had a pork shoulder for
Thanksgiving, and now we are having one for Christmas.
The hog only has two shoulders."

That was some of the sweetest meat that had ever been tasted.

Holiday Meat

Barbecue smoked, grilled, braised

Chicken, beef and ribs

Hickory, charcoal and fire

Secret ingredients for the sauce

A splash of alcohol and vinegar

Few drops of this and that

With a little salt and pepper

Mopped in the right amount of spices

Dripping in tangy sweet goodness

As varied as the styles of preparation

It must be the holidays

Communication Rules

If you want to talk to me
Make an appointment

I will have the first word
I will have the last word

I reserve the right to interrupt you
However, you may not interrupt me

I am always the winner
Even if I am wrong

These are the rules
For communicating
With the old folks

Declaration

Never permit
An individual
To tell you
That you are
As great as
They are

Rather declare
To them that
They are just as
Great as you are
Tell them that
They may see you in heaven

If they can make it there

Relocation

One day Papa looked down the dirt road.

He noticed that the woods were closing in on him on each side.

Pine trees were taking over.

Papa told Mama we have to get out of these woods.

We moved right in front of a cemetery.

Our home was the only house on the road.

He purchased two acres, and I purchased one acre next to him.

The house was torn down and rebuilt with the same lumber in the new location.

This was the third place Papa owned in his lifetime.

It was where he lived when he died at age 85.

Hope for the Hood

Of the places we choose to live
Our home is still in the hood
Life may not be fair at times
But our God is always good

Structures may crumble to the ground
As we struggle to find ways to cope
Circumstances beyond our control
Our community still resorts to hope

Often we miss what we never had
Then we lift our voices to complain
Peacefully protesting for our dignity
Hoping our efforts won't be in vain

We fight to hold our heads up high
Even in the midst of our sorrows
We keep the faith and hope alive
For there'll be better tomorrows

EUROPE
Shakespeare's Globe Theatre
London, The United Kingdom

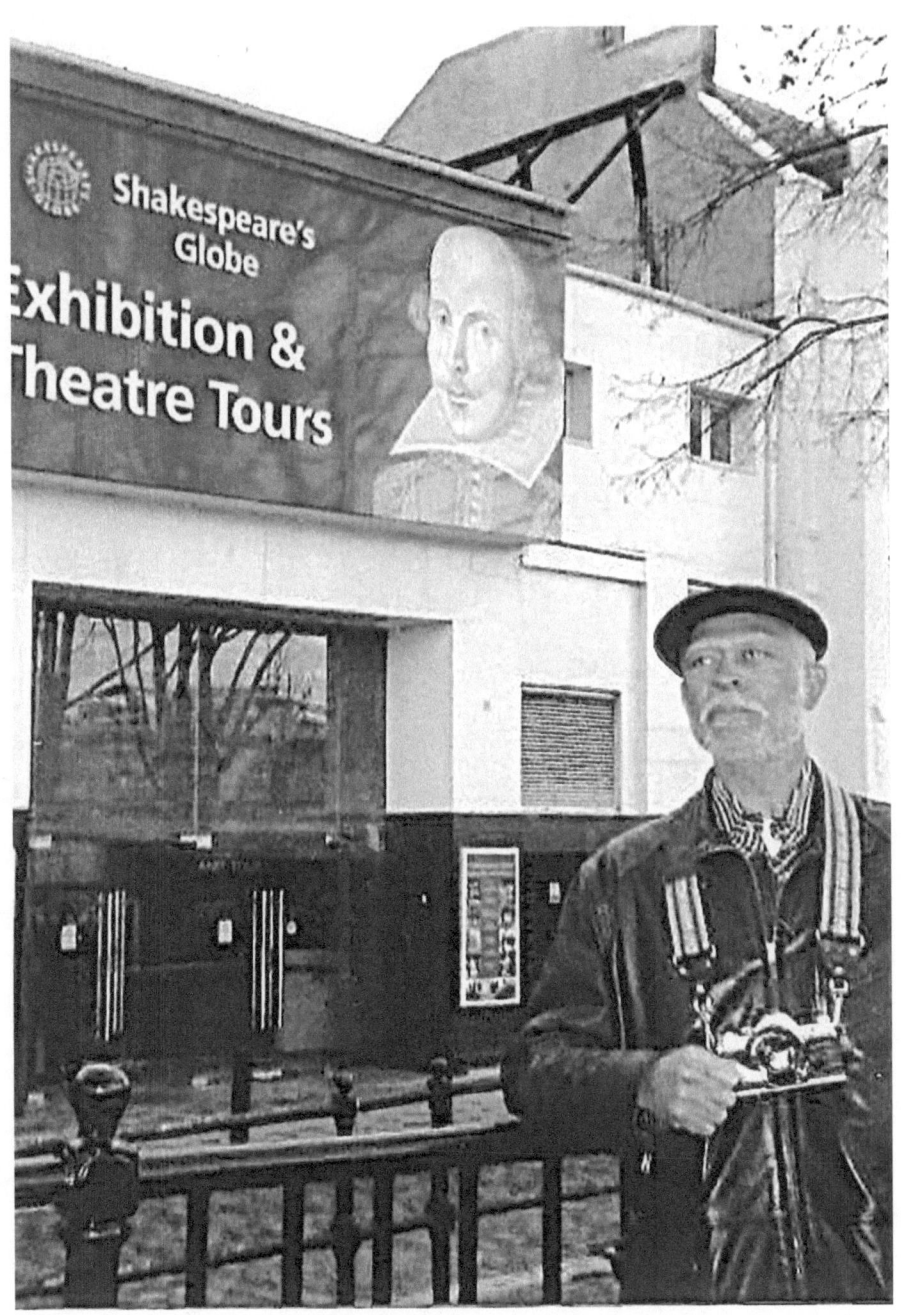

Elmer Beard

Paying homage to the Bard

Morning Chores

Early in the morning, I would rise
For my morning chores

I'd head to the barn
Horses were fed their breakfast
A half gallon of grain
And a block of hay

After my chores were complete
I'd climb in the barn loft
And take a nap in the hay

While back at the house
Breakfast was being
Prepared for my family

Nightmares

I was asleep in public.

Everyone was moving around me, but I could not move.

I called out to my son. He acted like he couldn't hear me.

I called out to my nephew, and he ignored me.

I hollered, "Help me!" But no one paid me any attention.

Then my daughter came and yelled at me, and I woke up.

I got in the tub and stayed until the water got cold.

I dried off and finished a couple of word puzzles.

I read my Bible and went back to sleep.

Tired.

A New Dog

Back in the late 1940s, we got a dog named Rover from a relative.

Throughout the week, he used to greet a white man who used to ride a horse by our house.

Then one day, Rover went out into the field and came across some 'coon poison and died.

Then Tip came along. Tip was a gift from a white man.
This was the same white man on a horse that used to
be greeted by Rover.

Rover couldn't greet the white man anymore because he was dead.
The white man felt sorry for us Colored kids, so he gave us a new dog.

And we named him Tip.

That Old Cat

We called that old cat Jim

A member of our family

We never bought him food

He ate what we ate

He came in and went out

Through a hole

In the screen door

When we moved

He moved with us

Didn't take too well

To the new place

Could've been the smell

Or the type of lumber

That old cat left us

Traveled three miles

Crossed creeks and streams

To get back to the old place

But we weren't there

Out of the Box

Challenge the system

Set a new precedent

Go against the grain

Swim upstream

Break the rules

Be different and odd

Be strange and unique

Be extraordinary and unusual

Be your own person

Don't get boxed in

Don't get trapped

Climb out of your comfort zone

Step outside of your box

Turn around and seal it shut

Then introduce yourself to you

In Lieu Of

They missed their chance

Instead of giving and sharing

Holding on to their worldly possessions

Counting their blessings

As they share not with others

Owning a clear conscience

Ignoring their community

Exercising short memory

While enjoying their abundant life

Some people who have more

Than they could use

In their lifetimes

When they leave they should not forget

Those who are left behind

They should share more

While they are here

Before their days are done

In lieu of later

Do good now

Mother Big Oak

College buildings sprouted around her
Once she was an acorn planted in the soil
Now as 150 years have blossomed

She is tender and tough as red oaks grow
Her roots so deep, her branches so wide
With leaves providing cool shade

For all those who gathered within her reach
She sheltered many students over the years
Four generations passed in her lifetime
She was the setting for precious memories

Our hearts broke like her withered branches
When she was uprooted and hauled away
A piece of us left with her

Chopping Block

Remembering those days in old Jim Crow
When backwoods were rural wonderlands
When Sista Mae was working, chopping wood
When other kids were running, playing games
A white girl made an unexpected appearance
Boldly placing her finger on that tree stump
Politely, Sista Mae issued the girl a warning
Before the continuation of her daily chores
The white girl did not heed her advice
The chopping resumed

Remembering that day in old Jim Crow
When Mama's worst fears became her reality
When eyes were closed and heads were bowed
When flashing lights came down the lonely road
White men in suits made an unexpected appearance
Thoroughly examining the blood-stained tree stump
Rudely, the authorities issued Sista Mae a warning
Before the evacuation of the girl with a nub
Silence fell over the rural wonderland
The praying resumed

AFRICA
W.E.B. Dubois Memorial Centre
Accra, Ghana

Elmer Beard
Researching history in the motherland

Magnetism

I believe the best of us is still within
I have one need, and you have another
Let's overcome challenges that divide us
So we continue to attract each other

Magnetism draws me nearer to you
Then you'll be nearer to me
Let us magnetize ourselves
Acknowledging our chemistry

May we sanitize our souls
May we forge magnetic connections
So we may love each other
And love all our imperfections

Brief Separation

They were arguing about

The best way to go home.

She threatened him saying,

"I'll get out of the car and walk."

He pulled over to let her go.

She opened the door and went.

He drove away.

She stood there in pitch darkness

On a country road in 1954.

After a moment,

He circled back for her.

She got in the car and sat

Speechless on the way home.

Sitting in the back seat

I wondered,

Why do they act like that?

Our People

Our people
Need to be reminded
That the struggle for justice
Freedom and equality is not over yet

Our people
Should tell the truth
About the way things are
About the inequalities that exist
And implicit biases and overt injustices
That have haunted us since we arrived here

Our people
Have to challenge
The system and hold it accountable
For decades of racial oppression and exploitation
We must educate ourselves so that we can educate others
Teaching accurate history even if it's uncomfortable and painful

You People

Notably distinct

Different species

Not like we are

"You people" are that

Undesired among us

"You people" don't fit

Stay in your place

Or go back home

"You people" sing

"You people" dance

"You people" run

"You people" jump high

"You people" want to be us

We don't want to be

"You people"

Pay Your Debts

Since you owe so much

Please pay your debts

It's your time to serve

Give your time or talent

Your dues are past due

Late fees will be waived

If your debts are paid today

Underground Banking

They had money in the Roaring Twenties.

But they buried their money in the ground.

Didn't believe in banks.

Banks failed. Banks failed them.

The stock market fell. And boom!

This was the start of the Great Depression.

There wasn't much great about it.

Penal Systems

Problems

Pain

Punishment

Pipeline

Prison

Parole

Probation

Powerlessness

Peril

Without Cameras

Citizens are armed and on patrol
Wrong is wrong and right is right
Without cameras charged and ready
Brutality would be out of plain sight

They say all stories have three sides
Officer narration is accepted as truth
Without cameras charged and ready
There's no case without visual proof

Humanity should always be adhered
Officer accountability is in dire need
Without cameras charged and ready
There's no justice without a live feed

Keep smartphones glued in your hands
Turn them sideways to get a fuller view
Without cameras charged and ready
Transparency blurs when it's only blue

NORTH AMERICA
The Old Homeplace
Chidester, Arkansas, USA

Elmer Beard
Revisiting the family estate

Well Water

In 1942, Papa dug a 40-foot well
Just a left-hand stone's throw
From the back porch

Relieved us from carrying
Water from the spring

One-half of the well
Was made of dirt
The other had a wooden wall

Sand seeped into the main stream
Regular cleaning allowed
For the bucket to fill itself
When it was lowered into the well

During the 1950s, the old well
Was covered with debris and trash

Today, it's just a hole in the ground
On the site of the old homeplace

My Mules and Me

Big, strong and often slow
Five times the strength of man
Black, brown and red in shade
And a few of them were tan

"Woe" to their well-trained ear
A list of commands they learned
"Gee" to the left, "Haw" to the right
Come up, get up, go, stop, turn

After plowing, hauling and pulling
Many miles they toiled every day
Drinking after me in the same spring
Then I would feed them a bale of hay

Donkeys and horses mix their genes
Bringing a dangerous breed to life
Never once did they endanger me
Stubborn but caused little strife

I tightened the bits in their mouths
Kept their coats brushed and combed
When they would stray off the estate
My mules always found their way home

Call My Name

As our Savior

You keep us safe

From the storms of life

In times like these

In our daily walk

In a world of sin

You uplift us and

Keep us anchored

Help us to improve

Our relationship with You

As we near the end

Of life's journey

When our day comes

For us to leave this earth

May our souls be at rest

And peace with Thee

When it's Your time to call

And my time to answer

Call me by my contract name:

Servant

And I will answer

Don't Call Me Bud

Don't call me Bud.

That name is reserved for close friends.

We are not close. We are not friends.

You barely know me.

If you knew me, you would show me respect.

You would call me Mister.

You would address me as Sir.

You would not call me Bud.

Buds are seedlings, incomplete objects

On their way to becoming what they are.

I already am who I am.

Fully formed, whole, mature

With a spirit, mind, body and soul

Save your efforts to be friendly to me.

Call me by my name.

Don't call me Bud.

Ode to a Landmark

As an aging beauty, a century-old
She's the essence of an era gone by
An architectural gem in the Classical Revival Style
In an array of brown and red bricks
Her columns and moldings in hues of pale gold

Black-owned and Black-designed, she stands four stories tall
For decades, her massive structure has served multiple purposes
Headquartering famed African-American institutions
Namely, the Woodmen of the Union and
The National Baptist Convention, USA

She was the nation's largest Black-owned bathhouse and sanitarium
Her thermal springs came rushing in at 140 degrees Fahrenheit
Just like those hot springs pumping through the national park resorts
That banned Colored people while falsely claiming to bathe the world
When it was she who bathed Black America

Catering to the upper echelon of African-American society
She offered a high-end haven during Jim Crow
Her front doors opened to celebrated entertainers
Educated professionals, civil rights figures, religious leaders
And Negro League players and famous athletes

Count Basie, Bill Bojangles Robinson and Duke Ellington
Were only some of her legendary guests and performers
Attracted to her impressive entertainment and conference venues
With a 2,000-seat auditorium, theater, gymnasium and dining hall
Attached to her 75-room accommodations

Intended to offer the most services of any complex of its kind in the South
She welcomed through her front doors Colored folks from all walks of life
Clients, customers, patients, teachers, students, preachers, congregants
Patronizing a Black-owned insurance firm, printing press, newsstand
Beauty salon, auto-body shop and shoe-shine corner

In her history, she had been a medical retreat healing Colored patients
In a hundred-bed hospital when public facilities turned them away
Black doctors and dentists opened private practices there
Including her training facility for Black nurses
Her therapeutic massages improved the community's overall health

She was the gathering place for the cream of the African-American crop
Affectionately, she was referred to as the National Baptist Building
Where we prayed our prayers and praised our Lord
We danced our dances and sang songs written by us
We were proud of her because, at the time, she was all we had

In the segregated South, she was a beacon of excellence
Centering Black culture, religion, politics, education and healthcare
She was many things to many people at many times during her life
She struggled to survive integration, marking her slow demise
Ailing, she fell into years of disrepair and neglect

Gentrification efforts attempted to level her to the ground
Like her neighbors that once lined a strip of bustling Black businesses
Today, she's alive and thriving, restored in modern-day grandeur
Providing affordable housing to her cherished senior citizens
She is a historical landmark in a district forever known as Black Broadway

Future Plans

Compose your own obituary

Write a will regardless of its legality

Pay for your funeral expenses in advance

Draft a guest list for your memorial service

Create a seating chart to avoid family tension

Select an appropriate song list for the occasion

Plan the order of service with tentative speakers

Buy a new outfit that will be flattering in your casket

Make a registry of suggested charities in lieu of flowers

Choose a color theme in advance for your guests to wear

Appoint someone to direct traffic and parking at the service

Designate someone to make the fried chicken and potato salad

Consider writing a witty caption for your headstone

Inform your family if you want to be cremated

Square things up with the Lord—today

Around the Casket

To mend broken family bonds
Must interventions be divine?
Relatives remain at a distance
Separated by silence and time

They don't talk; they don't speak
They don't really communicate
When they finally decide to reunite
It very well could be too late

Often there are confrontations
When our beloved one passes
Facing difficult conversations
As we gather around the casket

Too many regrets over the years
While sincere apologies too few
They have done what they did
Haven't done what they didn't do

With so much precious time wasted
Here's a question, if we dare ask it
If we decide to get together again
Will we gather around the casket?

Elmer Beard
The Octo Griot

BIO

Elmer Beard is a poet, author, retired educator, and lifelong freedom fighter. He is the former Democratic Election Commissioner of Garland County, Ark. He also served eight, two-year terms as a Hot Springs City Councilman.

An Arkansas native, Beard is the recipient of the 2021 Governor's Arts Award for his debut poetry collection *Let Reason Roll: Race, Religion & Reflections*. His first book, *The Challengers: Untold Stories of African Americans Who Changed the System in One Small Southern Municipality*, was a grant recipient from the Clinton Family Foundation, the Arkansas Humanities Council, the Arkansas Black History Commission and the Oaklawn Scholarship Foundation.

He has a B.A. in English from Arkansas Baptist College in Little Rock. He earned an M.S.E. in English education from Henderson State University in Arkadelphia. He also studied at the University of Wisconsin in Madison and the University of Missouri in Columbia.

Beard was supposed to spend his retirement traveling with his wife of 40 years. When she died at 65, his adult daughters invited him to travel the world with them. To this day, he has visited more than 20 countries on six continents.

At 87, Beard released his second volume of poetry, *We Didn't Come Here to Stay*, which is inspired by his journeys in life and his journeys around the world. He is affectionately known as the Octo Griot. The "T" is silent.

He can be followed on social media at www.instagram.com/octo_griot.

www.ingramcontent.com/pod-product-compliance
Lightning Source LLC
LaVergne TN
LVHW091535070526
838199LV00001B/78